George MacBeth was born in Shotts, Lanarkshire, in 1932. His family later moved to Sheffield, where he went to King Edward VII School, winning a scholarship to New College, Oxford, where he read Greats, taking a First in 1955. Joining the BBC that year, he worked as a radio producer until 1976, and was responsible for many broadcast series, including *The Poet's Voice*, *Poetry Now*, *New Comment*, and *The Lively Arts*. For the last fifteen years of his life he worked as a freelance writer and editor.

He was married three times and lived at various periods in Richmond, London, Hawaii, Norfolk, and finally in Co. Galway. He died, after a year suffering from motor neurone disease, in 1992.

He published the first of his many collections of poems in 1954; his last, *The Patient*, was published posthumously in 1992. He also published several novels, children's books, and edited several anthologies, including *The Penguin Book of Victorian Verse* and *Poetry 1900 to 1975*.

George MacBeth was a recipient of the Geoffrey Faber Memorial Award. *Poems from Oby* was a Choice of the Poetry Book Society, and several other of his books were Recommendations.

George MacBeth

Selected Poems

Edited by Anthony Thwaite

Preface by Carol Ann Duffy

ENITHARMON PRESS

2002

First published in 2002
by the Enitharmon Press
26B Caversham Road
London NW5 2DU

www.enitharmon.co.uk

Distributed in the USA and Canada
by Dufour Editions Inc.
PO Box 7, Chester Springs
PA 19425, USA

ISBN 1 900564 18 1

British Library Cataloguing-in-Publication Data.
A catalogue record for this book is available
from the British Library.

Typeset in Bembo by Servis Filmsetting Ltd
and printed in England by
The Cromwell Press

PREFACE

I first met George MacBeth on 29 September 1973, the day W. H. Auden died. George, then a BBC radio producer, had rounded up a handful of poets (Adrian Henri and Edward Lucie-Smith among them) enjoying an afternoon glass of wine at Bernard Stone's Turret Bookshop in Kensington and I went along for the ride. It was, I was later to realise, entirely typical of George that he would know exactly where in London on a Saturday afternoon to find enough poets to bundle into a cab, whizz across to Broadcasting House and coax into an instant radio tribute to mark the passing of England's greatest poet. The man I encountered in the Green Room, dispensing lavish gins and tonics and proffering boxes of BBC cigarettes, was slim, elegant, foppishly dressed in waistcoat and cravat, with a drawling (or *dwawling*, as he would have pronounced it) light Scottish accent and a moustachioed face that was alight with mirth, hedonism and subversion.

George MacBeth was an astoundingly prolific poet throughout his life, publishing, it seemed, a collection a year along with numerous pamphlets. His poetry is eclectic, formally dazzling, gleefully experimental. It is also continually drawn back to the traditional in form and is – particularly in his last poems of divorce and illness – painfully and honestly human. Like all poets, George MacBeth had his preoccupations and his work can show an interest in cruelty and the erotic on the one hand, war and heroism on the other. This new selection of his poems, long overdue since his sadly premature death from motor neurone disease, shows his generous ability to entertain, challenge and move his readers.

When poets are alive, they are able to keep their poetry in the public eye at readings and festivals, in schools and theatres, on radio and on television, at book signings and glittering prize ceremonies. When George MacBeth was alive there was no poetic gathering worth its salt round the tequila which wasn't graced with his presence. He was, always, a huge encourager of younger or newer talent and there are many poets in their thirties and forties today – myself among them – whose first radio broadcast was at George's invitation or who were introduced by him at the King's Lynn or Charterhouse Festivals, to name only two. I loved meeting George MacBeth through all the seasons of the poetry year and I love his poems. I hope that new readers will catch much of the nature of his talent and the spirit of the man within the following pages.

CAROL ANN DUFFY

SELECT BIBLIOGRAPHY

A Form of Words	Fantasy Press, 1954
Lecture to the Trainees	Fantasy Press, 1962
The Broken Places	Scorpion Press, 1963
Penguin Modern Poets, 6 (with Jack Clemo and Edward Lucie-Smith)	Penguin, 1964
A Doomsday Book	Scorpion Press, 1965
The Colour of Blood	Macmillan, 1967
The Night of Stones	Macmillan, 1968
A War Quartet	Macmillan, 1969
The Burning Cone	Macmillan, 1970
Collected Poems, 1958–1970	Macmillan, 1971
The Orlando Poems	Macmillan, 1971
Lusus	Fuller d'Arch Smith, 1972
Shrapnel	Macmillan, 1973
A Poet's Year	Gollancz, 1973
In the Hours Waiting for the *Blood to Come*	Gollancz, 1975
Buying a Heart	J. Jay, 1978
Poems of Love and Death	Secker & Warburg, 1980
Poems from Oby	Secker & Warburg, 1982
The Long Darkness	Secker & Warburg, 1983
The Cleaver Garden	Secker & Warburg, 1986
Anatomy of a Divorce	Hutchinson, 1988
Collected Poems, 1958–1982	Hutchinson, 1989
Trespassing	Hutchinson, 1991
The Patient	Hutchinson, 1992

NOTE ON THE CONTENTS

Between 1954 and 1992, George MacBeth published more than twenty books of poems, and many poems separately in the form of pamphlets and broadsheets. The books include two volumes of Collected Poems. This selection draws briefly on his first book (*A Form of Words*, Fantasy Press, 1954), the contents of which go back to his precocious late teens and early twenties. It ends with several poems from his posthumously published *The Patient* (Hutchinson, 1992), all of them written during the onset and swift progress of motor neurone disease.

The selection does not draw on some book-length sequences from which it seemed impossible to select without damage: *A War Quartet* (Macmillan, 1969), *The Orlando Poems* (Macmillan, 1971), *The Cleaver Garden* (Secker & Warburg, 1986), or the prose-poems of *My Scotland* (Macmillan, 1973). This book also excludes a number of pieces which George MacBeth made familiar to many audiences at poetry-readings during the 1960s and 1970s, such as 'Pavan for an Unborn Infanta' ('AN-AN CHI-CHI/ AN-AN CHI-CHI'), performance-pieces which, dazzling and hilarious at the time, need the memory of his performance to re-create them.

The attempt has been made to select, in their proper chronological order, a full and true representation of this prolific, inventive, skilful, moving and entertaining man's poems.

Penny MacBeth and I are very grateful to Carol Ann Duffy for her generous introduction to the selection, a characteristically warm response to a gifted writer who was also acknowledged by many (from Philip Larkin and Ted Hughes to Peter Reading and Ian Duhig) as a brilliant and selfless promoter of other people's talents.

ANTHONY THWAITE

CONTENTS

for Lally and George

Rhubarb

Two thousand years beyond their time
Untutored in the art of scope
These plants repeat an old mistake.

Flora now buried under grime
Once healed the first expansive ache
And threw their drowning world a rope.

But vast exceptions past their prime
On wasted ground without real hope
Still like to grow for growing's sake.

When sense of Taste controls the route
Plain Choice, avoiding paradox,
Derives its metaphor from fruit.

Most men who govern life by clocks
Like apples to be ripe and sweet
So choose the Worcester, shun the Cox.

But some who pause before they eat
Without a dash of cream in June
Scorn strawberries as incomplete.

And some born with a silver spoon
Surrender all their dates to chance
Or stone plums at the plenilune,

Some praise tradition, some advance
The prior claims of fashion, some
Favour a superstitious trance.

The mob still works by rule of thumb.
Dependent on their speed of grab
The strong survive, the weak succumb.

But private cliques condemn the drab
And emphasizing taste acquired
Strike out obliquely like the crab.

'The walnut has been much admired.
The shell is tight, the kernel warm,
The fibres neatly braced and wired.'

Is this applause for classic form
Or simple scientific pride
Applying physics to the storm?

Since either case proves choice denied
Bad rules of conduct clearly may
Result in mental suicide.

Preventing this, reform today.
Reject the sharp convenient knife
And prize the connoisseur's delay.

Facing the diametric strife
Between the quick gulp and the slow
Reflective savouring of life

Settle your views and strike your blow.
The flavour of the tangerine
Will show you to which side to go.

Shop therefore, criticize, be keen.
Walk round the stall and ask the price
Even of goods that look too green.

With daring you may soon entice
Desires extravagant or mean.
But first learn how to shake the dice.

You're all right with the Japs. I mean you've got
Your slant eyes and your cheekbones, for a start.
Then there's your pigmentation. I should say
You can't go wrong with Japs. It might be tan
If they were coloureds, but you're pretty safe
With Japs. Of course, you can't be too cock-sure

Or you're in trouble. Once you start to think
Some might be Chinamen, you're sunk. So don't.
What it boils down to is just this: you might
Feel you can tell by how they kick. You can't.
They come by at the same speed, one by one,
And they all kick the same way, more or less,

Unless they're lame. The heel-hooks don't allow
Much variation. And the running chain
Keeps them in line. You can't discriminate.
You have to treat them all alike. White's black,
Black's white in Liberty Hall here, gentlemen.
If they've got frizzy heads, well, what's that prove?

They might be catholics. They might be Boers.
They might be Jews. You can't discriminate.
The only thing's to treat them all alike
Or you'll get snarled up every time. Make sure
The blade's well-oiled and you can reach the lever.
That's what counts: not what shape nose they've got.

It makes no odds. You're here to do a job
Not let your prejudices run away
With you: they've all got good red blood.
Just pick the ones out you'd most like to use
When they go by. And don't let feelings in
Or you'll mislunge. One tip: it's wise to keep

To small men. You'll get tired soon enough
Jamming those buttons down. Conserve your strength.
Take a rest when you're tired. Don't get involved.
There'll be plenty more to try tomorrow.
I think that's all. You there: give me your knife
And let's go down. We'll have a trial run.

The musk-ox is accustomed to near-Arctic conditions. When
danger threatens, these beasts cluster together to form a defensive
wall or a 'porcupine' with the calves in the middle.

Dr Wolfgang Engelhardt,
Survival of the Free

I found them between far hills, by a frozen lake,
   On a patch of bare ground. They were grouped
In a solid ring, like an ark of horn. And around
   Them circled, slowly closing in,
Their tongues lolling, their ears flattened against the wind,

   A whirlpool of wolves. As I breathed, one fragment of bone and
      Muscle detached itself from the mass and
Plunged. The pad of the pack slackened, as if
      A brooch had been loosened. But when the bull
Returned to the herd, the revolving collar was tighter. And only

   The windward owl, uplifted on white wings
      In the glass of air, alert for her young,
Soared high enough to look into the cleared centre
      And grasp the cause. To the slow brain
Of each beast by the frozen lake what lay in the cradle of their
      crowned

   Heads of horn was a sort of god-head. Its brows
      Nudged when the ark was formed. Its need
Was a delicate womb away from the iron collar
      Of death, a cave in the ring of horn
Their encircling flesh had backed with fur. That the collar of death

Was the bone of their own skulls: that a softer womb
    Would open between far hills in a plunge
Of bunched muscles: and that their immortal calf lay
    Dead on the snow with its horns dug into
The ice for grass: they neither saw nor felt. And yet if

    That hill of fur could split and run — like a river
        Of ice in thaw, like a broken grave —
    It would crack across the icy crust of withdrawn
        Sustenance and the rigid circle
Of death be shivered: the fed herd would entail its under-fur

    On the swell of a soft hill and the future be sown
        On grass, I thought. But the herd fell
    By the bank of the lake on the plain, and the pack closed,
        And the ice remained. And I saw that the god
In their ark of horn was a god of love, who made them die.

THE DRAWER

Their belongings were buried side by side
In a shallow bureau drawer. There was her
Crocodile handbag, letters, a brooch,
All that was in the bedside cupboard
And a small green jar she'd had for flowers.

My father's were in an envelope:
A khaki lanyard, crushed handkerchief,
Twelve cigarettes, a copying pencil,
All he had on him when he was killed
Or all my mother wanted to keep.

I put them together seven years ago.
Now that we've moved, my wife and I,
To a house of our own, I've taken them out.
Until we can find another spare drawer
They're packed in a cardboard box in the hall.

So this dead, middle-aged, middle-class man
Killed by a misfired shell, and his wife
Dead of cirrhosis, have left one son
Aged nine, aged nineteen, aged twenty-six,
Who has buried them both in a cardboard box.

The Passport

Cleaning out old junk, I find
My father's passport, with his picture
Smudged with ink. The mauve-pink paper,
My name signed in his neat writing,
Eden's name there, make it strange.

He used it once, went on business
To Düsseldorf the year of Munich,
Brought me back a clockwork donkey
I still have and saw the war
Coming, which he fought in. Turning

The stiff pages in my hands, I almost
Feel his long-boned hands again
Over my child's hands. I wonder
What he'd think of my passport,
Wine-stained, full of stamps, uncancelled?

His eyes, questioning, look out
From under brushed-back hair. This man will
Never know I've been to Munich
Nor that our side won the war
Between our two journeys, our

Two lives. This draughtsman, born
At Overton in Lanarkshire
Late in 1904, whose height
It says is five foot nine, whose eyes
Are hazel, hair dark brown, is dead.

Baroque-handled and sharp
With blunt lead in their lips
And their fluted legs together
My father's compasses
Lie buried in this flat box.

I take it out of its drawer,
Snap old elastic bands
And rub the frayed leatherette:
It smells faintly of smoke:
The broken hinges yawn.

As I level the case to look
A yellowed protractor claps
Against black-papered board,
Sliding loose in the lid
Behind a torn silk flap.

I look in the base at the dusty
Velvet cavities:
Dead-still, stiff in the joints
And side by side they lie
Like armoured knights on a tomb.

One by one I lift
Them out in the winter air
And wipe some dust away:
Screw back their gaping lips
And bend the rigid knees.

In an inch of hollowed bone
Two cylinders of lead
Slither against each other
With a faint scurrying sound.
I lay them carefully back

And close the case. In Crookes
My father's bones are scattered
In a measured space of ground:
Given his flair for drawing
These compasses should be there

Not locked away in a box
By an uninstructed son
But like an Egyptian king's
Ready shield and swords
Beside his crumbling hand.

The Miner's Helmet

My father wore it working coal at Shotts
When I was one. My mother stirred his broth
And rocked my cradle with her shivering hands
While this black helmet's long-lost miner's lamp
Showed him the road home. Through miles of coal
His fragile skull, filled even then with pit-props,
Lay in a shell, the brain's blue-printed future
Warm in its womb. From sheaves of saved brown paper,
Baring an oval into weeks of dust,
I pull it down: its laced straps move to admit
My larger brows; like an abdicated king's
Gold crown of thirty years ago, I touch it
With royal fingers, feel its image firm –
Hands grown to kings' hands calloused on the pick,
Feet slow like kings' feet on the throneward gradient
Up to the coal-face – but the image blurs
Before it settles: there were no crusades.
My father died a draughtsman, drawing plans
In an airy well-lit office above the ground
Beneath which his usurpers, other kings,
Reigned by the fallen helmet he resigned
Which I inherit as a concrete husk.
I hand it back to gather dust on the shelf.

St Andrew's

Here in my tight suit, Sunday after Sunday,
I'd shiver in the draughty oblong hall.
(The fire-bomb-gutted church was never used
Except by children or for some church play
That needed ruins.) Here my pimpled skin

Wrinkled in prayer when I propped my head
On my poised fingers: forms of words worn thin
Helped me to remember what should be said.
I'd bend beside my mother, gangling, tall.
I prayed for faith, but felt that God refused.

Let me look back. I'm there in my rough chair,
Bare legs on sharp straw, sucking buttermint
Slipped in my fidgeting hands by fur-gloved hands.
I'm wondering when the intercession-prayer
Will end. More prayers, intimations, hymns

Flounce leisurely on. I watch bulged offering bags
Shuttle between deacons. Touched coins chink. Stiff limbs
Ease. The soft mouths, whose belly-velvet sags,
Gape for warmed silver, trickling out by dint
Of pressed appeals for 'our missions in far lands'.

The lesson booms out. James McClusky's black
Bony razor-headed bust above the bible
Strops his Highland vowels. Quick Scottish wives
Nudge their slumped husbands. Folded arms, feet slack
On loud planks correct themselves. The Book

Quietly shuts, gold leaves flutter. Towards
The back of the hall the text from Habbakuk
Re-echoes. The draped lectern's tasselled cords
Jerk to swung robes. The minister turns: the table
Quakes to beat fists condemning our distracted lives.

Let me look forward. As I grate on boards
I bump the lion-mouthed mahogany throne
He'd hunch in. It's ground by lecturers now. Dead flowers
Droop on the flat piano from which the Lord's
Thundering praises were wrung. I cough and choke

In dust (it's little played now) and stoop through
To the new church: too elegant in oak
For my taste. I advance to our old pew
Through pipe-warmed air. I sit down, scrape fresh stone
With dragging nailed heels. Here, while quarter-hours

Flake from the tower, I stop. My child's belief
(I now believe) was a Scots exile's; gone
With loosened roots. When the sick wish returns
For the lost country, the dream-Scotland grief
Was noble in, I clutch at things, plain things

I've lifted to symbols: compasses, a brooch,
Photographs, draughtsman's T-squares, opal rings.
My faith's planted where prayers can't encroach.
I've grown past God-roots. Why, then, back there on
That warm pew do they prick me? Something turns

Time back. It's Easter Day. I see moved plates
Of diced white bread, starched linen someone clears.
The plates clink closer. Furtively, I choose
Christ's body and blood. The hushed young elder waits,
Then catfoots on. And now I'm swallowing wine

From a glass thimble, rolling the lifeless bread
On my living tongue. I'm keyed for some sure sign
Of something miraculous. Eyes blink; my head
Lifts; and I stare at grown men shedding tears
And my own goosefleshed knees, blue with a bruise.

What did I learn at Greystones, my first school?
Something from clay. I don't mean garden clay
My father sliced like fudge-lumps, broken fudge-lumps,
With a steel spade's-edge. I mean clay for playing with,
Squelching-wet, white stuff: clay mashed flat like dough
On sweating palms; dried hard in brittle spindles
Between slow fingers; caked on backs of hands
Plunged wrist-deep into whitewash in grey clay-bins
Jammed in an art-room's corner to cludge it out.
Clay taught me filth. And what did tar teach me,
Stuck to my shoes' greyed lozenge-patterned rubbers
On the baked asphalt of our melting playground?
Tar taught what fire does. Before war broke out
I'd seen a trapped boy terrified by fire
Forced by six others in a smoke-filled cellar
And kept there coughing, choked with swirling ash;
And another crouching with his tight knees browned
With diarrhoea, blubbing behind the backs
At being nicknamed 'stinker'.
My uncle died floundering through Belgian sludge
In the First World War: my father died in fire
Charred in a Sheffield blitz. Through filth and smoke
Forgotten links with those blood-ridden soldiers
Educate my will. In clay and tar
Two wars collide: fouled bodies from my childhood,
War as the art-room clay, as playground tar,
Sharpens to that boy choking, that boy jeered at:
Tears, diarrhoea: what being burned, being dirty means:
That's what I learned at Greystones, my first school.

I own four knives that were made for killing. They decorate
    my house. In romantic moods
I picture myself accosting a burglar with one of them. First, a
    Victorian bayonet. This
One took a hell of a lot of guts to handle, I'll bet. It's a heavy thing.
    You can wrench

It in and out of its sheath, but it calls for a certain amount of sweat.
    I've crossed the two
I think of next like swords on my dining-room mantelpiece.
    First, a diminutive fruit-knife, marked
'Enthumion', Greek for 'a gift', for the classical tourist: a neat little
    scissor for slitting

An adam's apple. Some kind of juice has rusted the crescent steel.
    It sticks when it slides
From its wooden sheath. And second, my Scottish dirk. It's encased
    in a frayed-cardboard, Cameron-
Tartan holder. I clean its hilt's chased silver once in about six
    months. The dirt's

Ingrained like ash in the curling crevices. The blade has a diamond
    section. It's sharpened
On both sides like an axe. Given a cool head and a steady hand
    you could use
It for peeling potatoes. I don't. The last one's a lightweight ivory
    'Chinese' throwing-knife. The tip's

Broken off. And there's dried blood on the blunt edge and the
    words 'Meet Me at Maules'
In copper-plate. There are thirty-eight uneven slots notched in
    the hilt. All men
It's killed, I'd like to think. I wonder why I preserve these four
    not very important knives

I never use or clean. To give them space for decay in a decent
    slowness? In guilt
For a cushioned, inhibited life? I avoid their implications:
    they decorate my house
Through which I walk in the warmth of my five electric fires
    secure from the need to kill.

All day to the loose tile behind the parapet
The droning bombers fled: in the wet gutter
Belly-upwards the dead were lying, numbed
By October cold. And now the bloat queen,
Sick-orange, with wings draped, and feelers trailing,
Like Helen combing her hair, posed on the ledge
Twenty feet above the traffic. I watched, just a foot
From her eyes, very glad of the hard glass parting
My pressed human nose from her angry sting
And her heavy power to warm the cold future
Sunk in unfertilized eggs. And I thought: if I reached
And inched this window open, and cut her in half
With my unclasped penknife, I could exterminate
An unborn generation. All next summer,
If she survives, the stepped roof will swarm
With a jam of striped fighters. Therefore, this winter
In burning sulphur in their dug-out hangars
All the bred wasps must die. Unless I kill her.
So I balanced assassination with genocide
As the queen walked on the ledge, a foot from my eyes
In the last sun of the year, the responsible man
With a cold nose, who knew that he must kill,
Coming to no sure conclusion, nor anxious to come.

Who was here. Before his cat
Washed and rose. Without his shoes
Who inched outside while someone's hat
Made a noise. Light feet helped. Who's.

Whose are these eggs? Ladybird's.
Hard like crumbs of sleep. She flies
Off to help who find some words
For sounds and things. Who's two puffed eyes

Tug at flowers now for bees
Tucked away. Some try to hide
In pouting fox-gloves' jugs. Who sees
Their fat bear's thighs, though, wedged inside

Scouring honey. Look! Rare stones
In lupin leaves. Who's flapping gown
Shakes them all out. Ow! Who's bones
Aren't awake, make who fall down

Biting earth. Who hears a sound.
Whose are these wet softish hairs
Brushing someone's mouth? Can bound
As quick as you. Whoosh! Peter scares

A thin bird. Zip! Squawk! Its beak
Almost nipped who's fattest worm
Head and tail. Who hears him squeak
Through the grass: who sees him squirm

Down a hole. Who wants to kiss
His frightened worm. Who's coolish knees
Push him up to clematis
He thinks it's called. It makes him sneeze.

Gooseflesh comes. Who's bare toes rake
Up oily slugs. Who wants to hop,
Skip. Who's flopping tassels make
Ants run. Who hears his crispies pop.

MILDRED

Mildred, our batty cousin, 's been staying with us
Over the weekend. I'm worn out. On Friday
When Mummy and Daddy went to fetch her she wouldn't
Walk downstairs. Mummy said, 'Come on, Mildred,
Let's pretend we're bride and groom (shall we?)
And Daddy can be the bridesmaid.' It's always games
To make her do things, childish silly games
I'm sick to death of. She won't do anything
Without persuading. Do you know that twice
When the doctor made an appointment she was out?
Or she wouldn't see him. He'd gone specially
As a favour to us, too. Is she absent-minded
Or just contrary? Well, we don't know which
So we're keeping her locked up at home till she's seen
The psychiatrist on Thursday. Then she'll go home
Or into a home. Her body's cracking up,
Hospital might be better. She's had two strokes.
She's fifty-eight, but she moves as if she was ninety.
And she talks in this infuriating voice
You can't make head or tail of half the time
It's so slurred and slow. Then she's got kidney trouble
So you can imagine the state her flat's in.
No char would stay. And she's so bloody selfish
She'll fly off the handle at the least complaint
Or interference. 'Why can't I – come down
To the drawing – room and meet – people?' This morning
She wouldn't dress. Mummy had to put on
All her clothes: every single stitch.
And there's her money. The lawyer said for weeks
She's been drawing twenty pounds out every day
And then spending it. She bought a bubble car.
She bought this beautiful blue starred lino.
She buys yoghurt. We found twenty bottles

Of yoghurt piled up under her bed: all empty.
And about fifteen more unopened, half in
Half out of the fridge. All going bad, some stinking.
She'll spend a pound on lunch. At Coronelli's
This restaurant she goes to she leaves a pound on the table
And just walks out. I don't know what she's doing.
She'll sit there in the dining room after dinner
Staring ahead of her into empty space
Without looking at anything or moving.
Perhaps she thinks she's back in the theatre.
Theatres are what she's crazy about. Her husband
Victor was manager of the Globe. She goes
Four times a week to the pictures, sits in the front row
Wearing her best clothes, claps when the film's over.
We don't want to interfere: but the neighbours
Just take advantage. As things are she can't
Live on her own, though. And you couldn't have anyone
Living in: she takes such violent
Dislikes to people. She had this Italian woman
Marcellina, once. One day she actually
Threw her out: bundled her out of the door
With all her bags. She was the only one
Who was doing Mildred good. She made her work,
Help clean the place up. Ugh! I pity Granny
Having to sleep in her bed again. She's worse
Than Hank. I hope to God they find some grounds
For doing something definite on Thursday.
If we don't get her certified I'll go mad.

I'd say their marble cubicles were a shade
Too small for the taller men, but they all appeared
To be standing at ease. Oh the usual postures — hands
In their pockets, hands on their hips, hands on the wall.
A few touched themselves. A few were saying prayers
Perhaps. I expect a few were feeling the cold
From that bare cement floor in those bedroom slippers.
I did, in my shoes; but still, I suppose one allows
A little latitude in the provinces. No money
To do it all in style. However, it worked
And we did get going. One man was reluctant
To cooperate about buttons — a big fellow
With a lot of weight to throw around: it's always
Annoying that sort of thing: a nasty business
It can be on those tiles. So we gave a hand,
Igor and I. The locals didn't mind,
They rarely do. From there it was plain sailing
To the main business. The five attendants came
All according to the book, well-turned-out men
In their new aprons, with the usual hoses, and a good
Flexible pump. (I gave them marks for that. You know
There's a lot of friction on those grids if they scuffle
When you fit the neck-plates.
It might be worthwhile specifying cable,
Steel-strapped stuff; it would save in the long run.)
Fortunately, we didn't need it: they were all so docile,
Queued and shuffled out with no trouble at all.
Though the line-up was tricky — they'd done the count wrong
So we had to use the shoe-horn on a couple.
But after that it was fine: taps on,
Mask fitted, the legs well held, the right grip
And a nice simple injection — I always think
Those gas cylinders are all wrong. The infusion

Was one of the smoothest I've seen. Evacuation
Very decent. An infinity of freshness
In a little diffusion of bitter carbolic. Rather sweet.
It took about fifteen minutes to get the stories,
And not much mess: they had to scrub the channel
To clear some vomit, otherwise all OK.
No frills: but at least the operation was completed
With all proper precautions, the doors closed,
The men screened: and, oh yes, the windows open
To clean the air. I doubt if anyone smelled
A rat in the whole building, or heard as much
As a squeak from a plimsoll. They moved like professionals
From start to finish. I'd say it was all good work.
They certainly do things with the minimum fuss.
I'd recommend we exonerate the whole depot.

A True Story

When the British Association
For the Advancement of Science held
Its Annual Meeting one year in
    East Anglia no-one could

Think what to feed them on. It appeared
From previous experience in
County Durham that members consumed
    An enormous quantity

Of sandwiches. How were the hundreds
Of visiting scientists to be
Fed? The problem was finally solved
    By the inspiration of

A Norfolk poacher who suggested
At a public meeting in the Town
Hall at Norwich the employment of
    Their local pest the Coypu

Rat. He claimed that between two layers
Of freshly cut bread a thick slice of
Coypu tasted quite delicious. And
    It proved so. At any rate

The sandwiches were bought and eaten
In extraordinarily large
Numbers. The plain bread seemed to set off
    The unusual taste of

The dead rodent. Indeed a group of
Younger men from the Biology
Section dissected the furry beasts
    With a view to assessing

Just why. Altogether it was 'a
Great success for the quality of
Willingness to experiment' as
 The Countryman aptly said.

THE CRAB-APPLE CRISIS

for Martin Bell

To make this study concrete I have devised a ladder – a metaphorical ladder – which indicates that there are many continuous paths between a low-level crisis and an all-out war.

Herman Kahn, 'On Escalation'

LEVEL I: COLD WAR

RUNG I: OSTENSIBLE CRISIS

> Is that you, Barnes? Now see here, friend. From
> where I am I can see your boy quite
> clearly soft-shoeing along towards
> my crab-apple tree. And I want you
>
> to know I can't take that.

RUNG 2: POLITICAL, ECONOMIC AND DIPLOMATIC GESTURES

> If you don't
> wipe that smile off your face, I warn you
> I shall turn up the screw of my frog
> transistor above the whirr of your
>
> lawn-mower.

RUNG 3: SOLEMN AND FORMAL DECLARATIONS

> Now I don't want to sound
> unreasonable but if that boy
> keeps on codding round my apple tree
> I shall have to give serious thought
>
> to taking my belt to him.

LEVEL II: DON'T ROCK THE BOAT
RUNG 4: HARDENING OF POSITIONS

I thought
you ought to know that I've let the Crows
walk their Doberman through my stack of
bean canes behind your chrysanthemum

bed.

RUNG 5: SHOW OF FORCE

You might like a look at how my
boy John handles his catapult. At
nineteen yards he can hit your green-house
pushing four times out of five.

RUNG 6: SIGNIFICANT MOBILIZATION

I've asked
the wife to call the boy in for his
coffee, get him to look out a good
supply of small stones.

RUNG 7: 'LEGAL' HARASSMENT

Sure fire my lawn
spray is soaking your picnic tea-cloth

but I can't be responsible for
how those small drops fall, now can I?

RUNG 8: HARASSING ACTS OF VIOLENCE

Your
kitten will get a worse clip on her
left ear if she come any nearer

to my rose-bushes, mam.

RUNG 9: DRAMATIC MILITARY CONFRONTATIONS

Now see here,
sonny, I can see you pretty damn
clearly up here. If you come one step
nearer to that crab-apple tree you'll

get a taste of this strap across your back.

LEVEL III: NUCLEAR WAR IS UNTHINKABLE
RUNG 10: PROVOCATIVE DIPLOMATIC BREAK

I'm not going to waste my time
gabbing to you any longer, Barnes:
I'm taking this telephone off the

hook.

RUNG 11: ALL IS READY STATUS

Margery, bring that new belt of
mine out on the terrace, would you? I
want these crazy coons to see we mean
business.

RUNG 12: LARGE CONVENTIONAL WAR

Take that, you lousy kraut. My

pop says you're to leave our crab-apple
tree alone. Ouch! Ow! I'll screw you for
that.

RUNG 13: LARGE COMPOUND ESCALATION

OK, you've asked for it. The Crows'
dog is coming into your lilac

bushes.

Barnes. Can you hear me through this
loud-hailer? OK. Well, look. I have
no intentions of being the first
to use stones. But I will if you do.

Apart from this I won't let the dog
go beyond your chrysanthemum bed
unless your son actually starts
to climb the tree.

RUNG 15: BARELY NUCLEAR WAR

Why, no. I never

told the boy to throw a stone. It was
an accident, man.

RUNG 16: NUCLEAR ULTIMATUM

Now see here. Why
have you wheeled your baby into the
toolshed? We've not thrown stones.

RUNG 17: LIMITED EVACUATION

Honey. I

don't want to worry you but their two
girls have gone round to the Jones's.

RUNG 18: SPECTACULAR SHOW OF FORCE

John.
Throw a big stone over the tree, would
you: but make sure you throw wide.

RUNG 19: JUSTIFIABLE ATTACK

                              So we

threw a stone at the boy. Because he
put his foot on the tree. I warned you
now, Barnes.

RUNG 20: PEACEFUL WORLD–WIDE EMBARGO OR BLOCKADE

                    Listen, Billy, and you too
Marianne, we've got to teach this cod

a lesson. I'm asking your help in
refusing to take their kids in, or
give them any rights of way, or lend
them any missiles until this is

over.

LEVEL IV: NO NUCLEAR USE
RUNG 21: LOCAL NUCLEAR WAR

      John. Give him a small fistful
of bricks. Make sure you hit him, but not
enough to hurt.

RUNG 22: DECLARATION OF LIMITED NUCLEAR WAR

                    Hello there, Barnes. Now
get this, man. I propose to go on

throwing stones as long as your boy is
anywhere near my tree. Now I can
see you may start throwing stones back and
I want you to know that we'll take that

without going for your wife or your
windows unless you go for ours.

RUNG 23: LOCAL NUCLEAR WAR — MILITARY

                              We
propose to go on confining our
stone-throwing to your boy beside our
tree: but we're going to let him have
it with all the stones we've got.

RUNG 24: EVACUATION OF CITIES — ABOUT 70 PER CENT

                         Sweetie.
Margery. Would you take Peter and
Berenice round to the Switherings?

Things are getting pretty ugly.

LEVEL V: CENTRAL SANCTUARY

RUNG 25: DEMONSTRATION ATTACK ON ZONE OF INTERIOR

                         We'll
start on his cabbage plot with a strike
of bricks and slates. He'll soon see what we
could do if we really let our hands

slip.

RUNG 26: ATTACK ON MILITARY TARGETS

             You bastards. Sneak in and smash our
crazy paving, would you?

RUNG 27: EXEMPLARY ATTACKS AGAINST PROPERTY

                         We'll go for
their kitchen windows first. Then put a
brace of slates through the skylight.

OK.

Unless they pull out, chuck a stone or
two into the baby's pram in the
shed.

RUNG 29: COMPLETE EVACUATION — 95 PER CENT

They've cleared the whole family, eh,
baby and all. Just Barnes and the boy

left. Best get your mom to go round to
the Switherings.

RUNG 30: RECIPROCAL REPRISALS

Well, if they smash the
bay window we'll take our spunk out on
the conservatory.

LEVEL VI: CENTRAL WAR

RUNG 31: FORMAL DECLARATION OF GENERAL WAR

Now listen,

Barnes. From now on in we're going all
out against you — windows, flowers, the
lot. There's no hauling off now without
a formal crawling-down.

RUNG 32: SLOW-MOTION COUNTER-FORCE WAR

We're settling

in for a long strong pull, Johnny. We'd
better try and crack their stone stores one
at a time. Pinch the bricks, plaster the
flowers out and smash every last

particle of glass they've got.

RUNG 33: CONSTRAINED REDUCTION

We'll have
to crack that boy's throwing arm with a
paving stone. Just the arm, mind. I don't
want him killed or maimed for life.

RUNG 34: CONSTRAINED DISARMING ATTACK

Right, son.

We'll break the boy's legs with a strike of
bricks. If that fails it may have to come
to his head next.

RUNG 35: COUNTER-FORCE WITH AVOIDANCE

There's nothing else for
it. We'll have to start on the other

two up at the Jones's. If the wife
and the baby gets it, too, it can't
be helped.

LEVEL VII: CITY TARGETING

RUNG 36: COUNTER-CITY WAR

So it's come to the crunch. His
Maggie against my Margery. The

kids against the kids.

RUNG 37: CIVILIAN DEVASTATION

We can't afford
holds barred any more. I'm going all
out with the slates, tools, bricks, the whole damn
shooting match.

All right, Barnes. This is it.

Get out the hammer, son: we need our
own walls now. I don't care if the whole
block comes down. I'll get that maniac
if it's the last thing I – Christ. O, Christ.

I am dangerous
in a crisis
with sharp legs and a screw

in my genitals. I slice
bacon-rind for a living. At nights I
lie dried

under the draining-board, dreaming
of Nutcrackers
and the Carrot-grater. If I should

catch him rubbing
those tin nipples of hers
in the bread-bin

(God rust his pivot!) so much for
secrecy. I'd have his
washer off. And

then what? It scarcely pays
to be 'Made In Hamburg'. Even
our little salt-spoon

can sound snooty
with an E.P.N.S. under
his armpit. Even the pie-server

who needs re-dipping. In sixteen
stainless years dividing
chippolata-links I

am still denied
a place in the sink unit. And
you can imagine

what pairing-off is possible
with a wriggle of cork-screws
   in an open knife-box. So I

keep my legs
   crossed. I never cut up
rough. I lie with care

   in a world where a squint leg
could be fatal. I sleep like a weapon
   with a yen for a pierced ear.

Long long ago when the world was a wild place
Planted with bushes and peopled by apes, our
Mission Brigade was at work in the jungle.
    Hard by the Congo

Once, when a foraging detail was active
Scouting for green-fly, it came on a grey man, the
Last living man, in the branch of a baobab
    Stalking a monkey.

Earlier men had disposed of, for pleasure,
Creatures whose names we scarcely remember –
Zebra, rhinoceros, elephants, wart-hog,
    Lion, rats, deer. But

After the wars had extinguished the cities
Only the wild ones were left, half-naked
Near the Equator: and here was the last one,
    Starved for a monkey.

By then the Mission Brigade had encountered
Hundreds of such men: and their procedure,
History tells us, was only to feed them:
    Find them and feed them;

Those were the orders. And this was the last one.
Nobody knew that he was, but he was. Mud
Caked on his flat grey flanks. He was crouched, half-
    armed with a shaved spear

Glinting beneath broad leaves. When their jaws cut
Swathes through the bark and he saw fine teeth shine,
Round eyes roll round and forked arms waver
    Huge as the rough trunks

Over his head, he was frightened. Our workers
Marched through the Congo before he was born, but
This was the first time perhaps that he'd seen one.
        Staring in hot still

Silence, he crouched there: then jumped. With a long swing
Down from his branch, he had angled his spear too
Quickly, before they could hold him, and hurled it
        Hard at the soldier

Leading the detail. How could he know Queen's
Orders were only to help him? The soldier
Winced when the tipped spear pricked him. Unsheathing his
        Sting was a reflex.

Later the Queen was informed. There were no more
Men. An impetuous soldier had killed off,
Purely by chance, the penultimate primate.
        When she was certain,

Squadrons of workers were fanned through the Congo
Detailed to bring back the man's picked bones to be
Sealed in the archives in amber. I'm quite sure
        Nobody found them

After the most industrious search, though.
Where had the bones gone? Over the earth, dear,
Ground by the teeth of the termites, blown by the
        Wind, like the dodo's.

When I Am Dead

I desire that my body be
properly clothed. In such things
as I may like at the time.

And in the pockets may there be
placed such things as I use at the time
as pen, camera, wallet, file.

And I desire to be laid on my side
face down: since I have bad dreams
if I lie on my back.

No one shall see my face when I die.

And beside me shall lie
my stone pig
with holes in his eyes.

And the coffin shall be as big as a crate.
No thin box
for the bones only.

Let there be room for a rat to come in.

And see that my cat, if I have one then,
shall have my liver.
He will like that.

And lay in food for
a week and a day:
chocolate, meat, beans, cheese.

And let all lie in
the wind and the rain.
And on the eighth day burn.

And the ash
scatter as the wind decides.
And the stone and metal be dug in the ground.

This is my will.

Owl

is my favourite. Who flies
like a nothing through the night,
who–whoing. Is a feather
duster in leafy corners ring-a-rosy-ing
boles of mice. Twice

you hear him call. Who
is he looking for? You hear
him hoovering over the floor
of the wood. O would you be gold
rings in the driving skull

if you could? Hooded and
vulnerable by the winter suns
owl looks. Is the grain of bark
in the dark. Round beaks are at
work in the pellety nest,

resting. Owl is an eye
in the barn. For a hole
in the trunk owl's blood
is to blame. Black talons in the
petrified fur! Cold walnut hands

on the case of the brain! In the reign
of the chicken owl comes like
a god. Is a goad in
the rain to the pink eyes,
dripping. For a meal in the day

flew, killed, on the moor. Six
mouths are the seed of his
arc in the season. Torn meat
from the sky. Owl lives
by the claws of his brain. On the branch

in the sever of the hand's
twigs owl is a backward look.
Flown wind in the skin. Fine
rain in the bones. Owl breaks
like the day. Am an owl, am an owl.

THE RED HERRING

after Cros

There was once a high wall, a bare wall. And
against this wall, there was a ladder,
a long ladder. And on the ground,
under the ladder, there was a red
herring. A dry red herring.

And then a man came along. And in his hands
(they were dirty hands) this man had
a heavy hammer, a long nail
(it was also a sharp nail) and
a ball of string. A thick ball of string.

All right. So the man climbed up
the ladder (right up to the top)
and knocked in the sharp nail:
spluk! Just like that.
Right on top of the wall. The bare wall.

Then he dropped the hammer. It dropped
right down to the ground. And onto the nail
he tied a piece of string, a long
piece of string, and onto the string
he tied the red herring. The dry red herring.

And let it drop. And then he climbed
down the ladder (right down
to the bottom), picked up the hammer
and also the ladder (which was pretty heavy)
and went off. A long way off.

And since then, that red herring, the dry
red herring on the end of the string, which is
quite a long piece, has been
very very slowly swinging and
swinging to a stop. A full stop.

I expect you wonder why I made
up this story, such a simple story. Well,
I did it just to annoy people.
Serious people. And perhaps also
to amuse children. Small children.

The Ski Murders

AUTHOR'S NOTE

Consultants of this encyclopaedia–poem may find it convenient to work according to some arbitrary or appropriate programme dictated by a sequence of letters. These could either be meaningless, e.g., PZTE RFGN QQLX? or (perhaps better) grammatical phrases or sentences, e.g., 'WHO'S FOR TENNIS?' Naturally, one may want to apply the rule of one consultation one letter, so that in the example given the programme will be WHO'S FR TENI? A full reading of the encyclopaedia is not necessary to appreciate the main elements of the story, nor will complete acquaintance with the entries entirely solve the mystery. The ski murders remain the enigma they always were.

ANARAK: She felt his warm hand moving against the polished zippers of her pocket. In a moment the cold pouch would be opened, the photographs recovered. Gritting her teeth, she forced her head round and had thrust her shoulder against the laced front of his crimson anarak before the big man could turn. His gloved fist eased back and he grunted as his winded body fell in the hard snow of the toboggan run.

BLOOD PRESSURE: It was high, but she would live. Miles knew that. Through the glass wall of her centrally-heated bedroom he could see the black flicker of Z-cars (q.v.) in the sound-proofed *après-ski* lounge. Christ, he thought, when *will* they grow-up?

CORTINA: Inez dipped her cloth in the oil and gently drew it along the curved black blade. There was something sensuous, almost sexual, in this intimate washing and cleaning of such an immaculate and deadly implement. The straps into which her feet went, the long flat under-surface, the uptilted tip – she shivered at the thought of their caress on the crisp snow. Here in Cortina the symbolism of these instruments was appallingly close. She fingered her corduroy vole (q.v.) and lay back on the bloodshot candlewick of the bedspread.

DOUBLE DIAMOND: Cusumba was frightened. The thought of Prestwich's body down there in the sleigh-shed was on his mind. He ordered a second double diamond and watched the dark brown liquid froth from the can with a strange sense of achievement. At least he had not lost the power to order a drink. A Manx band struck up in the patio. He could hear the snow-owls in the pines. Life was a possibility.

EXPOSURE METER: It seemed to Prestwich as the old Rolleiflex gently bumped the *tête de nègre* behind his fair-isle cardigan that the best hiding-place might well be the least expected. He fingered the bakelite exposure meter in its calfskin holder. Here? Not forty yards away the Count was rehearsing his tournament chassis on the packed slopes of the ski-school.

FERGUSON: To the Count as he went down for the fourth time on the Chinese pye-dog the pocked leather case on the radiator was a mask of pain. Children's Hour (though how could they pick it up?) came out as a scream. de Montfort was buckling on his puce gauntlets for the *coup de grâce*. There was no time, the Count thought, there was no time. But he rose to his knees and, reaching with bleeding fingers for the tiny black box which could save him, switched the white disc onto Luxembourg. It was accident, but the foreign music stopped the blow.

GENETIC CODE: With his ice-axe Cusumba hacked the Third U in the wall of the glacier. Overhead he could hear the Sikorski (q.v.) circling. Those great battering wings! Like the yellow hornbills in the elephant's graveyard of the Congo. Would the Irish zeppelin be in time to read the message before the thaw? Already he felt the ice warm to his sweating cheek. He visualised the swollen gold cigar in the clear air of this last resort he had so loved. Raganza came to the mullioned windows of the gondola. He was holding his German binoculars. The black lenses tightened on the distant ice-fall.

HUYSMANS: Prestwich ran his nail-file across the rough white string of the package. It frayed, broke, curled away on the polished pine-blocks. He began to unwrap the heavy cartridge paper with a sense of mounting excitement. Any moment now he would hold the key to the genetic code (q.v.) in his hands. The book itself, when it fell at last from the underlying tissue, was a disappointment: slim, black, encased in cheap linsen boards. He turned it over in his stubby hands. Could this really be the answer to the problems of Ulster? (q.v.)

ILINX: The glass bubble spun on its metal wire. As she fought for breath in her gas-mask, Inez could see the world whirling like a storm of snow in a paper-weight. Her lashing ski-boot flung open the gilt-edged complete Huysmans (q.v.), and she watched the elaborate pages of *A Rebours* unfurl on the wet rubber as Ellington bent over her prostrate body. In a wave of dizziness she could feel the escalating roundabout of passion engulf her.

JEW'S HARP: The Count began to pluck absent-mindedly at the strings of his anarak (q.v.) as he climbed the ski-slope. In the spare pocket of his camera-case there was a small grey musical instrument whose purpose and name he had not yet learnt. His brows furrowed as he strove to remember the definition of a jew's-harp: could that be it? It would all fit – the bedraggled Kafka (q.v.), the doped Weetabix (q.v.), the alert face of Immelman in the helicopter.

KAFKA: Ninian accepted the consequences. As she fastened the little capsule against the glue-stiffened entrenchment of the spine, she wondered what Kafka would have thought. That sly, oppressed Czech, that justice-ridden Jew: how could *he* have known the agonies of the secret agent, the midnight hallucinations of the spy in the ski-resort?

LIGHTER FUEL: The Count squeezed the tiny rubber cylinder in his fingers. The plastic measurer lay glistening slightly in the candle-flame on the edge of his bed. He smelt the exciting, raw odour of petrol. Once, twice, he nipped the pierced end of the little container: and smiled grimly to himself as the bulging drops oozed and dripped into their slowly filling bath. Outside the window, Miles Ellington had moved the catch on his Derringer.

MINOX: The matt aluminium felt cool against his burning cheek. He lay in the snow and took it. Give or take five minutes the Italian police would reach the ski-station by seven o'clock. Beaumaris had a good start but he could never work the pedals in those clogs. Still, it was a good start. If only the first roll had been developed on Friday! That fourteenth shot of Ninian Rich in the deep end would do the trick. Thank God for the built-in exposure meter (q.v.), Cusumba thought, as he fell back on the vellum Kafka (q.v.).

NOSTALGIA: The film spread easily over her damp skin. Cool, glossy and crackling, it encased her bosom like a layer of varnish. They would never think to look for it there. For a moment she felt a stab of nostalgia for the old methods, the negatives in the bran barrel, the contact prints listed in a cigar catalogue. But the weakness passed. She was soon striding over the creaking boards of the tea-chalet towards the chair-lift.

OMO: The white suds bubbled in the lavender basin. Inez caught her creamed face in the glass. My God, she thought, what wouldn't I give to be a man for once. Her cool nails moved on the taut skin of her bust, slipped to the side, released the firm catch. In the pale orange light from the wall fitment Ninian watched the proud nipples lift and pout as their pink shell dropped in the foaming bowl. It was several minutes before she grasped the full implications.

PECCARY: de Montfort ground his teeth. In the Arnheim zoo once they had fed a peccary together. The fastidious little pig had come on high toes to nibble fudge from her hand. As the wind whipped his bared face in the darkness he began to count the years since anyone had touched his cheek as she had. Pull yourself together, man, he found himself muttering, there is work to be done for the people of Ulster (q.v.).

QUETTA: The little bastard just *might* have been born there, too. You never knew. No wonder the English were dying, Inez thought, as she felt once again the magnificent ilinx (q.v.) of the tumbling ski-lift: no wonder, when men like Prestwich were in control. She hugged her mink anarak (q.v.) tighter round her elegant shoulders and watched the sun glinting on the Count's skis.

ROLLEIFLEX: The body of Simon Prestwich lay in the smashed laths of the sleigh-shed. There seemed to be a smell of burnt cordite in the air. Miles knelt beside him, the revolver smoking in his hand.

The Rolleiflex they had come to know so well was broken open, the film had gone. Miles buried his head in his hands.

SIKORSKI: The great fans of the Russian helicopter beat the air. Through the snow-encrusted perspex Immelman could see the tiny black figure far below on the glacier. What was the stupid bastard doing there? He slipped the brown octagon of a zube between his teeth and crunched thoughtfully as his wasp-coloured machine hovered over the snow-fields. There was work to do here for the de-coding unit at a quick guess.

TETE DE NEGRE: Miles Ellington allowed the blade to sink at its own speed through the chocolate-studded ball on his plate. Very few of these were available at such lofty altitudes, he knew, and of those no more than a quarter were impregnated to the full with the real Spanish sherry he could so surely taste the flavour of in this one. He paused with the last morsel half way to his lips as the sound of a muffled explosion came to his ears. It had come from somewhere down there in the fir plantation.

ULSTER: What on earth were they doing it for, de Montfort asked himself in the freezing men's-room. For a one-horse republic in an under-populated island? Not even for that: for a two-bit dependency of the English Empire. As he drew the silver teeth together in his groin, a hair caught and he cursed, fluently, in Yiddish. Outside, the Irish lace of the snow fell like a judgment on the half-buried pages of *The Castle*.

VOLE: Inez Lawson-Emery had nothing on. Not even the radio, Cusumba reflected, as he pressed his bloodshot eye against the ivory key escutcheon of her bedroom door. In the nun-shaped aperture of cream and gold fur exposed to the eye the most striking novelty was the maroon corduroy vole on her dressing-table. Its beady eye stared fixedly into his own beside the superb coppery buttocks enthroned on their Danish leather stool. Now, he thought, and was through the door with his hand on the shutter as the long tanned body rose to its full height on the pony-skin.

WEETABIX: Of course, there would really have been eighteen to the packet: but Miles Ellington had other things to think about as he pasted down the cardboard flap of his elaborate decoy. Licking salt from his fingers he tipped the last spoonful of strawberry Yoghurt down his throat and rose to leave the table. That porrage-hating nigger was in for a thin time with his orange juice.

XENIA: Yes, it was there, once; at Nauplion, in winter. Nobody left but the regulars and Miles. I saw him first in the sun-lounge with his feet on a Moorish coffee-table, reading Huysmans (q.v.). We exchanged the usual greetings. I in my squalid pullover, he in his Chester-Barry two-piece. Over an ouzo we hatched The Plan.

YOGHURT: The little jar rested lightly in Ellington's bronzed fingers. Nothing disturbed the early evening silence but the click of spoons. He licked his lips. That stupid breakfast food would have to do the job. Cortina was hardly the place for gun-play. And that little affair of the Count's broken rib-cage had taken some hushing up. If only the old yobbo had learned to ski. With a single smooth movement the spy rose and turned as Cusumba's grin blockaded the doorway.

Z-CARS: Ninian slid her long legs one by one into the tight elastic sheath of her midnight blue stretch pants. There would scarely be room for an extra fountain pen in these, she reflected, as she studied the silent unrolling of Z-cars on the foreign screen. What use would sound have been in a language of which she knew no single word save the one for making love?

THE BAMBOO NIGHTINGALE

a funeral song to America, for her Negro dead in Vietnam

I rise like a wooden bird from China. I sing
    from the echoing bellies of coolies
in the rice fields. I mount on a curved gable
    in South Vietnam. I scream
across the Pacific to where you bask with your dolphins

in the riches of San Francisco. All down the coast
    your Golden Gate opens
to the poverty of Asia. I speak to the oranges
    rotting on trees. I address
the Bikini-strip of Sausalito, the beats

poising their chop-sticks. I make you the music
    of hunger and blood
crying for redress. America, listen. You have raided
    the inarticulate one time
too many. The reckoning comes. Below the pagodas

moulded in rain, your GI boots fill
    with the feet of centipedes. Your cowboy
politicians march on their stomachs into
    the supermarkets of mercy
without their credit cards. Your dandy aviator

posturing in leather gloves at his microphone
    inverts his torch each night
at the Hollywood Bowl of money. His witches' Sabbath
    sieg heils. And your army
of drafted ex-slaves fights out and across the ant-ridden

basin of the Mekong Delta watched over by the wings
    of helicopters. Out-generalled
by the Granddaughters of the Revolution, they die
    for the inalienable right
to six feet of Republican ground. At Forest Lawns

the suicide fringe of your Upper Four Hundred are laid
    to rest in velvet. Your war
heroes are buried in a field commuters pack
    their abandoned Buicks by
a mile from the Pentagon. A shrouded crucifix

exploits the Passion. Each apache heart
    has a stake in it, the Old Glory
catches the throat. I see your packed quiver
    of machine-stitched chevrons, the
Redwood aisles are your coffin timber. It is

the apocalypse of unequal rights. I hover
    with the eye of a newsreel camera
above the cortège of a black sergeant. My zoom
    lens pulls up his mother's
creased face into sweating ebony satin for

your moment of truth in *Life*. I caption her: *Jesus,*
    my boy was a white man
the day the reds nailed him. Remember that war
    when the limbs of your KIA airmen
formed up by fours again from their cold storage

in a Normandy abattoir. The Oxford hands
    reverently placed them back
in their air-cooled coffins, caring only what colour
    they were. America, here
the checkerboard squares of your white dream intermingle

in aerosol incense. Your soda-fountains are a-glitter
    with the nickel panoply
of the plastic Christian soldier. Even his screams
    are canned. You embark for crusades
against the marijuana-culture your fifth

column of Shanghai laundrymen in Buffalo
    smuggles in across the Great
Lakes. It is war to the needle against the yellow
    men the black men
are impressed to be targets for. The splinters of *Lightnings*

rust in the bones of North Korean villages
    nobody bombed except with
propaganda. Oh, exploding paper hurts
    only the graduate squaw
with her head in the schizophrenia of *Newsweek*. Truncheons

of Crazy Foam ooze from their cylinders
    in the All-white wigwams at Culver
City. Where is the doped brave with his hand
    burned in the embers of a New
Deal? The traffic cops in Alabama

bite on the bullet. Amphetamine is the mother
    of invention. Oh, come on,
America. The old con won't work
    any more. In the high-rise
incinerators of Austin Confessional Verse

can snipe itself to a Jewish cinder. Cry
    all the way to the bank while we cool
the Capone generation. The B-feature
    illusion is over. Your gangsters
have moved to the groin. Tonight is the massacre

in the under-trunk of clover leaves, the St Valentine's
    Day of the mobile gasoline
war. Vanzetti dies in the punctured sperm
    of your golden-armour-plated
Cadillacs. America, I smell your orgasms

in the copper exhausts of Mustangs. I taste your burned
    flesh in the sassy-flavour
of breakfast foods on W U O M. Your hypodermics
    have entered the marble temples
of Lincoln. In the scrapyards of Arlington

the Galaxie and the Continental are one
    tin. Its canisters
have unfolded their soup of blood in the clenched knuckles
    of the hard shoulder. Dip
your wheel into vomit, America. Spoon into flesh, the

cornflakes of Minnesota are deaf to the crackle
    of burning skin. I give you
the toast of Napalm. America, wring
    the brass neck of your melting-
pot. Hanoi is the cauldron of truth. Saigon is

the blazing Southern Cross of the Isolationist
    paradise. Ky is the killer
the Carl Sandburg village has no room
    in its penthouse for. America,
listen. The Goldwaterism that shelters your cold

executives in their minds of Samsonite
    has filtered the sun to a trickle
of ashes in light. Their mouths gape and scream
    for clay. Between them your body
they care about less than the clear glass in their eyes

is drained like a horse to make veal. Where now has the fury
of dried blood gone? ask
the Macarthurite bronze gods in the fought–over beaches
of conquered Iwojima
decorated by the sea. In the grey heart

of the University Section the heirs of Walt
Whitman are a mile high
on the morning glory seeds of electrodes clipped
to the genitals. The great
American epic rocks in the spilled bowels

of Dillinger. The internal war game
of mah-jong continues
by the yolk of human eyes. The monks burn
into silence. There is no one to sweeten
the acid policy in the porcelain

of your LBJ Acropolis. Call it the Black
House, if you like. It looks
that way to the dark sergeant whose brains were charred
with the legacy in the headlines
of the *Times of Pecayune*. His eyes are closed

to the peacock of the American rainbow. His ears are deaf
to the buzzing of W A S P S. His nose
is open to the stench of rotting corpses rising
out of the jungles of Hanoi
to corrupt the affluent. His mouth is twisted

with the sour flavour of black blood. His hands
are burned like an eskimo's
with the ice of not minding his business. America,
listen. This is the end
of the everlasting Charleston, the Wall Street crash

on the dollar merry-go-round, the dime hand-shake
        in the golden soup-kitchens
of disillusion. I weep for the onion-domes
        of the Kremlin. This is the bite
of iron. If you forget it your millionaires

will die in their X K Es for a brass thimble
        of Curaçao. The days
of the sugar economy are over. The guerrillas walk down
        your skyscrapers, beating
their steel breasts for the oiled virginskins

of Los Angeles. America, listen. Your body
        moves like a moth in the beautiful
stage of emerging from metal. Her chrysalis
        is the scrap-tide of iron. You advance
minute by minute towards the wheeled oblivion

of the killing-bottle. Take off your leopard-spot coat
        and bathe in the Yangtze river
with me tonight. There is no one to judge our battle
        except the future. I ask
for a striptease of guns. Lay aside your helmet and swim

for an hour in the moonlight. Perhaps beneath the willows
        in the evening cool of the water
some peaceful magic will happen. I ask you to move
        into the fluid of reason
below the lianas. I wait to bathe you in oil

or in blood. Answer me out of your prosperous iron
        in San Diego. Address
some message of sorrow to me in Saigon. Send
        your Pacific troubled with waves
of Oregon pity. Say that you hear and will come.

O English Food! How I adore looking forward to you, Scotch trifle at the North British Hotel, Princes Street, Edinburgh. Yes, it is good, very good, the best in Scotland.

Once I ate a large helping at your sister establishment, the Carlton Hotel on Waverley Bridge overlooking the cemetery on Carlton Hill. It was rich, very rich and pleasant. O, duck, though,

roast, succulent duck of the Barque and Bite, served with orange sauce, mouth-meltingly delicious! You I salute. Fresh, tender and unbelievable English duck. Such

luscious morsels of you! Heap high the groaning platter with pink fillets, sucking pig and thick gammon, celestial chef. Be generous with the crackling. Let your hand slip with the gravy trough, dispensing plenty. Yes, gravy, I give you your due, too. O savoury and delightsome gravy, toothsome over

the white soft backs of my English potatoes, fragrant with steam. Brave King Edwards, rough-backed in your dry scrubbed excellence, or with butter, salty. Sweet

potatoes! Dear new knobbly ones, beside the oiled sides of meaty carrots. Yes, carrots. Even you, dumplings,

with indigestible honey, treacle-streaky things. You tongue-burners. You stodgy darlings. Tumbled out of the Marks and Spencer's tin or Mr Kipling silver paper wrapper, warm and ready except in summer. Cold strawberry sauce, cream and raspberries. O sour gooseberry pie, dissemble nothing, squeezed essence

of good juice. Joy in lieu of jelly at children's parties, cow-heel that gives the horn a man seeing my twelve-year-old buttocks oiled in hospital by a nurse assured me, dirty old bugger. I eat my six chosen slices of bread, well buttered, remembering you and your successor the tramp who stole a book for me. Cracked

coffee cup of the lucky day, betokening mother-love, nostalgic. Fill with Nescafé and milk for me. It is all great, sick-making allure of old food, sentiment of the belly. I fill with aniseed's

parboiled scagliola, porphyry of the balls. With, O with, licorice, thin straws of it in sherbert, sucked up, nose-bursting explosives of white powders! Yes,

montage of pre-European Turkish delights obtained under the counter in wartime, or during periods of crisis, and

O the English sickness of it. Food, I adore you. Pink-faced and randy! Come to me, mutton chops. Whiskers of raw chicken-bones, wishes

and plastic cups. Unpourable Tizer. Take me before I salivate. I require your exotic fineness, taste

of the English people, sweep me off my feet into whiteness, a new experience. With beer. And with blue twists of salt in the chip packets. Grease of newspaper. Vinegar of the winter nights holding hands in lanes after *The Way to the Stars*. It

is all there. Such past and reticence! O such untranslatable grief and growing pains of the delicate halibut. The heavy cod, solid as gumboots. And the wet haddock, North Sea lumber of a long Tuesday's lunch. Fish and sauce. Nibbles and nutshells. Gulps of draught ale, Guinness or cider made with steaks. English food, you are all we have. Long may you reign!

I was born in Rome from the yolk of eggs
With a bit of mosaic between my legs.

In Byzantium, I was plated and screwed
Until they discovered *The Art of the Nude*.

Van Eyck was an early performer in flesh,
He laid me under a fine gold mesh.

Hieronymus Bosch had a fertile mind,
He blew me with a clarinet, from behind.

Leonardo was a sadistic bleeder,
I couldn't stand swans, so he made me Leda.

Brueghel was a vicious Flemish brute,
I was varnished by him in my birthday suit.

With Lucas Cranach, life was grim,
There were gropes in water, and then a hymn.

Tintoretto took me along a tunnel,
And a brace of disciples felt up my funnel.

Canaletto made me the colour of rum,
When he oiled my vagina it made me come.

Vermeer of Delft was the first voyeur,
I stripped for his mirror, to make quite sure.

With Rubens, it was the Sabine Rapes
On an apparatus like a bunch of grapes.

Anthony Van Dyck gave me VD
On the back of a sinewy horse, with a flea.

As for Boucher, that versatile frog,
He enjoyed me backwards across a log.

David, the bastard, gave me a dose,
And besides that, he was one of those.

Ingres, too, was inclined to be queer,
He tickled my nipples with a Roman spear.

With Delacroix it was chain-mail vests
And discharging his musket across my breasts.

In England, Rossetti soaped my belly
With what he called pre-Raphaelite jelly.

Burne-Jones needed the boots and hair,
His palette seemed blunted when I was bare.

With Auguste Renoir, I shared a punt,
Only things went blurred when he kissed my –

With Picasso I nearly did my nut,
I was taken to bits by him, in a hut.

As for Braque, with his *nature morte*,
I don't find all that corpse stuff sport.

With Salvador Dali, life was worse,
He had beetles crawling when I got the curse.

I died at last, a kinetic Venus,
And Jim Dine embalmed me in a polythene penis.

A GIFT

Returning from the car, I come late home
And hear you weeping through the closed front door
Before the key scrapes in the lock. In the dark
I see you sitting, halfway up the stair,
Curled in a foetus-shape as though in a womb,
Wearing your dressing-gown, striped red and gold,
As if for a ceremony not to take place,
Dressed up for birth, and still not to be born.

There are no words to show how much I care.
I go downstairs, close the door in my brain
On what seems too terrible to let out
Though it rips inside me. And then outside
In the quiet garden, behind the house,
I hear another sound, a scraping by stealth.
Turning, I reach to let in what I can.
I bring you the soft new hedgehog in my hands.

THE LAND-MINE

It fell when I was sleeping. In my dream
   It brought the garden to the house
And let it in. I heard no parrot scream
   Or lion roar, but there were flowers
And water flowing where the cellared mouse
Was all before. And air moved as in bowers

Of cedar with a scented breath of smoke
   And fire. I rubbed scales from my eyes
And white with brushed stone in my hair half-woke
   In fear. I saw my father kneel
On glass that scarred the ground. And there were flies
Thick on that water, weeds around his heel

Where he was praying. And I knew that night
   Had cataracted through the wall
And loosed fine doors whose hinges had been tight
   And made each window weep glass tears
That clawed my hands. I climbed through holes. My hall
Where I had lain asleep with stoppered ears

Was all in ruins, planted thick with grime
   Of war. I walked as if in greaves
Through fire, lay down in gutters choked with lime
   And spoke for help. Alas, those birds
That dived in light above me in the leaves
Were birds of prey, and paid no heed to words.

Now I was walking, wearing on my brow
   What moved before through fireless coal
And held my father's head. I touch it now
   And feel my dream go. And no sound
That flying birds can make, or burrowing mole,
Will bring my garden back, or break new ground.

The war is over and the mine has gone
   That filled the air with whinnying fire
And no more nights will I lie waiting on
   Cold metal or cold stone to freeze
Before it comes again. That day of ire,
If it shall come, will find me on my knees.

It occurred to Marshall
that if he were a vegetable, he'd
be a bean. Not
one of your thin, stringy
green beans, or your

dry, marbly
Burlotti beans. No, he'd be
a broad bean,
a rich, nutritious,
meaningful bean,

alert for advantages,
inquisitive with potatoes,
mixing with every kind
and condition of vegetable,
and a good friend

to meat and lager. Yes, he'd
leap from his huge
rough pod with a loud
popping sound
into the pot: always

in hot water
and out of it with a soft
heart inside
his horny carapace. He'd
carry the whole

world's hunger on
his broad shoulders, green
with best butter
or brown with gravy. And if
some starving Indian saw his

flesh bleeding
when the gas was turned on
or the knife went in
he'd accept the homage and prayers,
and become a god, and die like a man,

which, as things were, wasn't so easy.

ON THE DEATH OF MAY STREET

for my grandfather

You built it, and baptized it with her name,
Sixty-eight years ago. No angel came

That first Edwardian day to plant the stone
And make a child. Your wife conceived alone

And bore my mother in that soaking room
Where water later flowed, that choked her womb.

Tonight I write that May Street is condemned
And sure to die, as she was. Gripped and hemmed

By the sour blood of change, that rips and kills,
It dies far quicker than she did by pills.

I own it, and I see it broken, stone
By mother-naked stone. I heard her groan

That last night in our house before she died,
Not knowing how to help her. So I cried,

As I do now inside, to see her name
Shaken, and wasted. For your wasted fame

I cry to you, grandfather, in your grave
In rage and grief. All that you failed to save

Has shrunk to geometry, to crumbled lime
Beside the brickworks, to your grandson's rhyme.

THOUGHTS ON A BOX OF RAZORS

bought at a Stalham sale

I

For two pounds, they were mine. The price seemed right.
I thought of Housman's shiver, as he shaved,
And open sorrows that might cut the skin.

One razor curves beside me, black and clean.
It seems to swoop, when closed, as though in flight.

The hollow, bird's-beak-sectioned blade's engraved.
I touch its coldness, anxious to begin,

Watching the thirteen others as they grin.
Men's tender bodies are what razors craved.
I sense their famished hunger, their sweet bite,
Their glitter in ebony, obsessed, obscene.

And yet this glitter, with its power to stun
That seems so Japanese in these, looks trite.
It takes me back to Sheffield, and what's done.

II

Suppose I try to focus on just one.
This German GBNG, flecked with rust
And dated 1918, 's caught the sun.
Spread out across my page, its vague V-thrust

And hooking nose bring Dorniers to mind.
My war, that was. I hear old engines drone,
And civilians dying, with no testament signed.
That blitz was mine, I feel it as my own.

Others have carried razors, cold like this,
And stropped them sharper on strong leather thongs.
I touch my German friend. Its rustling kiss
Across my finger thrills like Chinese gongs.

I see the owner was E. Mann, my name.
My mother had one like this, much the same.

III

I go too far. I've jammed one in a churn,
A butler's cleaner for a carving-knife.
You shove a handle, and twinned rollers turn
And clear the blades of grease. In all my life

I never saw one till eight months ago
At an Aylsham sale. I bought the next I saw,
And cleaned it up. I use it now with dust
Of emery powder that's already in.

It's weak, but it works, with knives. A kind of crust
Will come off surfaces, and make things show.
I thought I'd clear the razor of some flaw,
But it caught inside. The blades of knives are thin,

A razor's upper section's far too thick.
This made the movement of that whole drum stick.

IV

Now I lay ten in a circle. Each has teeth,
Like cogs in an alarm-clock, and a groove.
As if relaxing, edges are in sheath,
And out of sight. They make a ring of steel,

Whose rim is ivory, whose hub is bills,
Or beaks. I mean the hooks you shift them by,
And make their sharkness arch with. As it moves,
You feel the irony. It eats and chills.

The irony that glisters in each eye,
Brassy and raised, is part of why they wheel
Into such penguin swimming forms. They fly
Only when open, vicious by the keel

That clears by inches the sea floor of time,
And leaves for grief deposits, bloody slime.

V

'Napoleon' seems much skinnier than the rest.
A trifle stiff-backed, and a smidgeon marred.
In the middle of his blade, he has a nick.
Old Nick. They might have called him that, for fun,
In Sheffield, England, where they carved his kind,
Those cutler brothers, John and William Ragg.

I see them in their sweat-shop, bony crags
Like stalwart men, with Elba on their mind.
They slaved, like Mr Stokes, like everyone
Who listened for the cold alarm-bell's click,
And took home hands grown calloused, and bone-hard.

These built Napoleon, by their chimney-breast,
And sent him far from Sheffield, to shave chins.
I tap their dread invention on my shins.

VI

Razors need razor-like precision. These
Don't quite have that. This boxful leans on rhyme.
I see the brook of recollection freeze,
And feel the cross of parting, like a crime.

I could abandon rhyme, though. Force a sly
Sixth-line decision to be less exact.
A sort of gear change, as it were, in fact.
That would be fluid, like a flow of thigh.

I don't suppose I'll do it, though, nor try.
Good rhymes can cut you. They can make you cry.

Remembering does that, too. So when I
Remember blue Gillette, and rusting blades,

A kind of guilty subjugation shades.
I see my father's car, and cases packed.

VII

Wearing these memories, in their common flight,
I take up three fresh razors, heavy ones
All black. I need the heft of weight tonight,
The drag of solid iron, like a plough's,

To upheave my brain. Ideas hinge and flee
At the solstice of a poem. They earn space
By how they touch me. Seconds out, I see
The reaching hands of grief, and her blank face.

The razors wait like rifles, nose to tail.
Like strips of hardened sword-blade, in a pail.
Like knights in armour, for their holy grail
Going to war, in coats of khaki mail.

Turning, I hear the sound of English guns.
I see my mother's tears. I touch her blouse.

VIII

I touched her blouse again when she was ill,
Feeling the curve. Razors have that, well wound
As if around some foreign hill. Great scythes
Don't hold the same allure. Scythes rake the ground

While razors float. They take our skin for tithes,
Winged surgeons. At our faces, with their fists,
They scrape and till, until the tissue breaks,
And leaves wide acres open to bare cysts.

The mother's curve, though. Is it this that makes
The elegance of swords from old Japan?
The simple shape of Time, drawn as a man?

I don't know. There's a straightness in their rule,
Razors. When I was nearly twelve, at school,
I used to want a razor that would kill.

IX

I never got one, though. I bought my first
At a garage sale in Saratoga Springs.
It's lying stiff, bone-yellow, much the worst
For wear, while all my rest make rings

Around it, on that empty cabinet
Whose lacquer top I'm using for their ground.
It's ominous, a tale of warring kings,
A nightmare game. How ten bright shiners rose

And trapped a colleague on their killing-mound.
Somehow I don't suppose the rest would set
Into a pattern slighter than I chose
If any sliced his neighbour into bits

And screeched away. I wonder, though, if it's
More razor-like to savage with no sound?

X

Once you get fantasy, what's left to say?
You get sheer viciousness, a misty sheen.
Imagine some girl murderously neat,
Stiff as a fish–bone sticking in your throat.

She takes a sharpened razor. To make sure,
She sharpens pencils. To make doubly sure,
Until those hexagons shed flakes of cones
She sharpens. Those are fir-tree's, these are hers.

She sees her man walk home from Stalham, gay
In his gaiety, and randy as a stoat.
It isn't easy to be quite so mean,
Even as she is, like a bitch on heat.

She does it, though. Cover the man with stones.
Bury this John Clarke's razor, with his bones.

XI

No true disciple of the modern world
Would aim to buy a cut-throat still to use.
Even a safety razor might seem odd.
Those brushes in the window, that arcade

Off Piccadilly, seem to stand for show.
Collectors might accept one, nicely curled
Into a smooth maroon case. Years ago
When all men lathered, in some louche decade,

It might have frightened you to read the news
Of a Sweeney Todd, a-swivel in your chair.
It wouldn't quite have marked one as a clod
Not to be shaved well, but, in good repair,

A gentleman kept razors. That was life.
As necessary as a decent wife.

XII

My father lost his, in a time of strife,
Long after he had gone. In middle age
My mother knew the worst, and what she said
Stays with me now. The Royal Hospital

Had instruments laid out on moving trays,
Like razors. Did they shave the nightly dead,
And lay them empty in each well-made bed?
This is the memory that slowly slays,

The sight of screens. What happens with the knife
Behind those frills must happen to us all
In years to come. And it's good cause for rage,
That frictive rage against the dying light

I feel seep through these handled, broken forms,
And rake in agony, like icy storms.

XIII

Downstairs I hear the heater moving. Tired,
I know it's after eight, and time to eat.

You will be cooking, standing by the stove,
Slicing potatoes, carrots, from your crate.
The table may be laid. And silvered blades,
Planted for eating, ordered by each plate.

They'll take my mind away from these retired
And scandalous old razors. Quite as neat
As razors, in much straighter lines, knives store
Bold energies of peace, of summoned awe

Our quiet house provides. By natural law
I ought to honour this deliberate grove
Of stainless trees. But, no. Knives have it made.
I prefer razors, they do rougher trade.

In sadness, I feel inspiration fail.
I bought these cut-throat razors in a box
With a wireless, and a metal case for coins.

I didn't need them, I just like old blades,
And things to keep things in, symbols of loins
Psychiatrists would say, the spike and hole.

But it's really more than that. I like these locks
Along the money-case, and on my chests,
Even if they don't close. I like the shocks,
The tingling brinks, of razors. In this house,
I falter sometimes when I touch your breasts.

I have to try again. To keep things whole,
In all we do, it helps to think of raids,
And live with a Sheffield edge. Wholeness is frail.

TO PRESERVE FIGS

for Iseult

Go up the whitewashed ladder, by the wall,
                And you'll find seven pounds
Of them, half-ripened, on the tree.
                The rest were low
I picked before. They wallowed free
                Near to the ground's
Welter of nettles, apples, weeds. I know,
        You'll have to take care. You might fall.

But there are plenty, seven pounds I'd say,
                Still floundering heavy, green
And solid in the August air,
                And you can reach
Them if you climb. So go up there
                And get them, keen
As fig-juice in your envy. Gather each
        Into your fingers, let none stay,

On the branch. It makes a metaphor for lust,
                This grasping for the rounds
Of unripe figs that ooze their juice,
                Their sperm. It burns,
That juice, and has no helpful use.
                You'll live with mounds
Of severed energy, with jaded urns
        Whose milked white necks you'll have to trust

Through all your life. It's best you learn that soon.
The acid in the fruit
Prickles the world with its pain
And nothing breaks
The dour addiction of the brain
To what may suit,
Or spoil. So watch your mother while she makes
These tractable. Take up a spoon

And help. Three times they boil, and have to steep,
Then boil again. Three times
It always has to be. So let
Them dry in trays
In your burning oven. Go and get
A sugary slime's
Blandishing oil. In winter, black to your gaze,
Like whales from arctic ice, they'll leap.

November at the Piano

for my mother

Not able to play, I touch your keys with the unskilled tips of my
    fingers, feeling a tune. The music
Echoes to the edge of the world. From the kitchen, the smell of a
    good dinner prowls, encountering my nose.

All senses coagulate. Holding the yellowed strips of ivory down, I
    squeeze out a last
Resonance from the hammered strings. It sings like a dying fly into
    corners of dust where vases

Of laurel abandon their petals. The delicate flavour of chord upon
    discord settles. The savour of hope
And melancholy in the balance of high and low that is all I can
    manage mingles. Outside the long window,

November is gathering force. In the sweat of the gale, my great
    beech-tree is sewing the grass with fire. I dwindle
Into another mould, a minute excrescence of tiny sound as I plunge
    my finger onto

A sharp note, slicing it off, like a breath of onion, or dry smoke. I
    remember your hands
As I touched them once, over sinks and baking bowls, and in power
    along such keys as these. I salute

Your competence in my ignorant feeling. I use my nose and my
    ears, under my hands, to arouse my mind.
I shall never play the piano, as you could play it, or cook, as you
    could cook. I can only

Suffer the sense of trying, hearing the sound, smelling the odour.
    This first November here
In my chosen Norfolk, what seems to matter is to ground your
    place in my echoing house, and to blaze your skills.

Mother, I need to remember, I need to feel. I have only these three
    senses to reach and hold
You with. Let me see your face in the fallen leaves. Let me taste
    your blood in the apples down from our trees.

The need to find a place always returns.
In Richmond, where my eighteenth-century bricks
Fashioned an avenue to stable skin,

I built a proper house. At Holland Park,
That fleece and leather took their comfort from,
I tried another, in another way.

Both worked. And what the simple martyrdom
Of wanting some position broke for sticks,
And set in place, held back the creeping dark.

I turned there, in my darkness, on my beds,
In tiny rooms, alone, and with my wives,
Or girls who passed for wives. And all my burns

From being lonely, and unsatisfied,
Flared in the silence, like a sheen from tin.
I waited, and, while waiting, something died.

Then, in the heat of Norfolk, I found you.
You brought the sun, through darkness, to my hives,
The bolted iron to my crumbling sheds,

You changed the whole world's shape. Your power grew,
And I, in feeling that, wanted some place
More generous for it than those gentle homes.

I needed somewhere with a flirt of grace
To match your fervour for long acreage.
I found it, here at Oby. Naked space

Over the cornfields, and the next-door farm,
Contracts to an oasis with great trees
That north-east winds can ravage in their rage

And leave still rooted and serene. In these
I feel the sweep of beech-wood, like an arm,
And something deeper, in our copper beech.

That brings a birthright in its massive reach,
A sense of giant time. Seeing it blaze
In widespread feathering, I feel the past,

The creak of longships on the Caister shore,
The swing of mills beside the easy broads,
And something closer, groping slow, at last,

The pleasant rectors, knocking croquet balls.
I take their heritage, and what it pays,
And vow today to make its profits pour

Through founded channels, in my well-kept grounds,
As growth, and preservation. Nothing falls
Or sings, in this wide garden, but its sounds

Calm me, and make our full liaison rich.
So my dream-Scotland grief was noble in
Will drag its graves beneath these grounded urns,

And stake its base in watered Norfolk clay,
And Kinburn be reborn, as what it was,
And my grandfather, and our Springer bitch,

Both live, in their own way, and like it here,
And feel the rain and sunlight on their skin,
And no one tell apart, which one is which,

The dream of former grandeur, and the firm
Everyday presence of our daily lives.
This is my hope, and what these lines affirm.

THE LEVERET, IN THE TWILIGHT

for Iseult

You found him beside the wall,
on his side, in the sun.

The long body laid sideways,
the great legs bent.

I touched what seemed the still-warm,
heaving fur,
watched the brown eyes, like small dates,
the black-tipped, fluted ears.

He was dying, even then.

I got a cardboard box
from the dairy,
and turned him over
to see if he was wounded.

There was only a trickle of urine,
like clear water.

We put him in the tack room
in the afternoon darkness
with the door locked against the dog.

He lay, without moving,
in a bed of straw and ruined leaves
balanced above the cold floor
on a set of folding deck-chairs.

And there he must have exhausted his coma,
and given back what was given to him
in his own time.

I don't know when.

He may even still be alive
as I write these lines,
hearing the rain beat on the south window
in the wind,
as the May night seeps in early,
the long season of spring dying
beginning as usual.

One last thing
I remember now
in the warmth of my study
is the way you crossed yourself
as if to avert what had to come.

I think of Cowper,
mourning his lovely pets.
I think of the little, round-nosed vole
the cats took this morning.

I think of that long darkness
creeping out of the west,
and of you, Iseult,
eight years old, on Tuesday,
who found a dying hare, in the sun,
for your birthday present.

THE PLACE

Sometimes, if I look back, I see the road
And high suburban houses crowding down
Towards the gennel, and then Bingham Park
As a presence at the bottom, green with trees.
It makes a crescent, a strange rising curve
That loops back round in swallowing itself
Like a sort of buckled belt. Through each front door
The little hall runs through, and through the kitchen,
To a stone plateau, a kind of flight of steps
Protected by iron railings from the drop.
You could stand outside there, and look all round.
Nothing was happening, and everything.
But how much was real? I mean really real,
Enclosed all round by brick and pebbledash
With fences, dropping lawns, and shrubbery?
I don't know. Something blurs whatever comes,
And a kind of sad fear sifts between the stones.
I can't tell memories from photographs.
Granny in black, and Smuts, whoever Smuts was,
And my father's Humphrey-Bogart-looking hat,
They're all the same, determined by being in albums.
I have to start elsewhere, if anywhere.

THE 1914 PARTY

Across the lawn a long parade of girls
With buttoned gloves convey unpassing time
And underneath the beech, a wide skirt swirls:
   Far out, like rhyme.

Dressed as a major in some abstruse corps
With Sam Browne belt, and crowns upon my sleeves
I slap my bulging cords, not worn before.
   No one believes

My kind of officer. No pips or gun,
Or any polish on his riding-boots,
And my sword-frog and flask are worn for fun.
   If someone shoots,

His make-believe loud shell will make a bang
And faze the ladies, twirling parasols.
Not one of us could march a parasang
   Or fill with holes

A can of beer set up upon a cart
At fifty yards. I stroll, and would salute,
Though rather warily, what might impart
   A distant hoot

Of laughter, a real military man,
This proper major, eighty-six years old,
Stiff on his stick, with keen eyes and a tan,
   Whose fire's grown cold.

Medals come easy, like this DSO
Whose colours nip my undeserving chest
But his were his. Yes, that was long ago,
   And that seems best.

But still, inside my head, becapped and grey
With middle age, I think a fine salute
And make it stick. We play a game today
        But it takes root.

And in my mind, remembering that war
My father died in, and the one that's done,
Or may be done, this game is played with awe.
        And what's begun

In quirky humour, ends as reverence.
The women furl their things. It starts to rain.
And the Edwardian age, bought for some pence
        And a frill train,

Is drawn indoors. There sepia photographs
Of Wilfred Owen, and of Hemingway,
Who wears his helmet proudly, but still laughs,
        Preserve our play

And set it in a frame. I turn and pour
Another glass of port for someone new
In ordinary clothes, who likes my floor
        And wants the loo.

Outdoors in the garage, a frail red cross
Indicates where our dressing-station lay.
My old wound stirs, that massive sense of loss.
        It comes to prey

On all I have. Whenever I'm alone
It grips with claws at what I cannot be,
One of those dead who gave past war its tone
        And made me, me.

I watch the tears of water on the pane
Outside the library. I hear the birds
Chatter in fear, as I twist round my cane.
          Words are just words

And these, though mine, change nothing. All this year
The seasons have prolonged forgotten growth
And flowers budded, and my death grown near,
          And we are both,

Lisa and I, set forward in a way
That may preserve the best, and, should we die,
Still honour all the braids of yesterday
          And hold them high.

This feels a duty. To receive our boons
And rinse them, torn like colours from the past,
And, as with these forced rituals, mark some runes
          And nail them fast.

A little soldier watches through your cot
    In a black busby, and red coat.
    His outstretched arms, wedged through the cane,
Attract your eye, perhaps, as these things can.

I wonder, though. While dozing, both eyes shut,
    Against the towel of your sheet,
    Have you, alongside your left knee,
Another soldier, whom you never knew,

Living in how the flesh bends, and the hair
    Drifts backwards from the warm skull here?
    I like to think so. And that soon
These echoes of his time that kept me sane,

The faltering mementoes of my drawer,
    When shown to you, will not seem drear
    Or meaningless, but something prized,
And by your gesturing, fine hands appraised.

The night that you were born, an unknown nurse
    Knitted this present. It seemed nice
    At first, and now more real, though frail,
Than any lace around your cot, or frill.

A soldier for a soldier. This for one
    Whose fingers of a Scottish wain
    Can grasp the softness of a war
And learn what heritage he has to wear.

My father's uniform was dull as mud
    Not like this pretty wool one made
    In colours, but of khaki serge
Whose beaten honours no grief can assuage.

I tell you, Alexander, my young son,
    Whose body now must keep me sane,
    That one day later, bound by blood,
Your conscience will salute all those who bled,

And there, amongst them, cherish your near line
    By being what you are, alone
    Out of that massive sea, your clan,
The one remaining soldier, weak and clean.

THE JUDAS TREE

Somehow betrayal simmered in the air,
    Took roots, and made a tree
    With round leaves. As I walked out there
Under the turrets, watching, we made three,

You and I and the Judas tree, grown sheer.
    The sun set flaming in the west
    Beyond the church, and night strolled near.
I thought that planting something would be best.

So, wet in wellingtons, I dug a hole
    And opened the dry boats
    The seeds had come in. April's mole
Will feel their sprouting on his velvet coat's

Resilience. You will be back by then,
    Ready for life and spring.
    Italian gold will shrink. This den
Of icy worth will glitter like a ring.

Meanwhile, I trowel earth. A failing sun
    Tips into fenny mire.
    Indoors I light white cubes, and one
By one they blaze to make a bitter fire.

Where were you last night?
Don't answer. I
Know where you were.

What was his name?
Don't answer. I
Know his name.

No, I don't want to know
Who you weren't with. When
I say you were
With someone, that's where you were.

Pass me the tongs.

You were where
I say you were, weren't you?
That's better.

Why were you there?
I know why, but I
Want to hear you say why.

The jug.
Swallow this.

Now tell me
Why you were where I don't
Want you to go.

Why you go there
With someone you know I don't want you to go with.

No, I don't want to know. I
Want to hear
The sound of my own voice going on and on.

Going on and on and on and on and on.

Tear out her tongue.

That's better.

THE POSTMAN

Past a green hole in the wall
With VR on it,
He drives his orange van.

'In the 1920s
You wore a bottle round your neck,
If you couldn't speak English.'

Is that so? Thus Matt,
The Republican postman
Who brings me letters from England,

Smiles through dark glasses,
His peaked cap
A reminder of military glory.

Nothing smiles
More easily than victory
On the former landlords

Who still wash their Jaguars
Before the portals
Of an Irish excellence.

But who cares? Not me
Nor the educated postman
Who remembers Patrick Pearsse

And can recite his poems
In a language
Neither Yeats nor Wilde could speak.

THE IMPOSSIBLE GUEST

Imagine the impossible guest:
His hair is greasy, he speaks mainly Spanish,
He behaves like a Nazi.

So far, so bad. Add in that he smokes,
Including during meals, a foul pipe,
Apologising, and asking if you would get him an ash-tray.

His cases, which you have carried from the station
On the hottest day of the year, O.K.
So that wasn't his fault, but it doesn't help,
Are tartan rexine, and stuffed with pornography.

His telephone calls, after midnight,
On your phone, to his wife,
Are long, loud, and recriminatory.

Your grasp of Spanish is just enough
To pick up, ear ground to the key-hole,
That he isn't arranging the date of his flight home.

Most of the time he seems, and is,
Drunk, on your Guinness. He breathes crumbs
Over the Norfolk jacket you have bought him
Out of a sense of guilt for the olden days.

After all, he was something else then,
A hell of a lad, as you were,
A real shit-raiser.

Then, wham.

He mentions, quite casually,
During a candlelit dinner, that he has multiple sclerosis.

Red faces all round, yes?

But you still pay the two hundred and forty-nine
Irish quid, and ship him back
Fast, to his pad in the west. It seems best.

I mean, for Christ's sake,
What else can you do
With a snoring farter
Who ogles your friend's wife?

Damned if I know.

The degenerative process advances fast.

Good afternoon. So good
Of you to have come. Here we all are.

This is Fiona, my grand-daughter, she's
Making a box
For her douroucouli.

This is Alaric, my grand-father, he's
Cleaning his pipe
Into a jam-jar. He's rather deaf, I'm afraid.
AREN'T YOU, OLD FELLOW?

This is Edwina, my wife's
Lady's maid, she's
Percolating coffee, in a colander. Will you
Have some?

This is Hengist, my
Faithful hound, actually
He's a bit of a mongrel, a bit manky.

And what's he doing? I think he must be
Spring-cleaning his equipment.

Who is this, darling? Ah yes, this
Is Roger Longrod, who
Does the drains. Thank you, Roger,

There's no need to shake hands.

And this is Pipistrelle, the
Baby-sitter, she
Rocks Fiona to sleep every night
With her krumhorn.

This is the drawing-room, and this
Is the room
For folding newspapers. Mind the drip,

That's Edgar, paring his nails. A cousin, yes.

Anyway, there you have it. Lorimer Hall
In all its glory. I look
Forward to your book, especially the photographs
Of the dove-cotes and the footmen's loo.

Mind the caravan, as you leave,
In the drive. We have a visit
From Oonagh, my mother-in-law.

And this is her family, yes. They deal
In scrap metal. All fourteen of them.

Sorry about the mess
And your exhaust. But they're easily replaceable,
Aren't they?

Do come again, when you've time
And the energy. We'll do the cow-byres, too.

And where were you the night
We burned Mount Sion? Were
You in the passing crowd, or safe
At home in Ballyruin?

That's me in the cloth cap, Declan,
Your old father's father, seventy years
Back, near as damn it. I was
Up there by the colonnades.

        I remember,
I remember, all those beer-flushed faces,
James and Paddy, Rush and Edwards, all
Ploughed under like the landlords.

        Who
Was there, was Jimmy Daly, Jimmy from the forge? Was
He there?

        I don't know, lad. I
Remember curtains blazing, plaster breaking, taken
All in all, it was a fine night, better
Than a football riot.

        Meanwhile, far away in London,
Lord and Lady Simper-Footwell, stuffed their hearts
With spit and mustard, largely ignorant
Of what was happening, idle at some Chelsea Ball.

Good riddance to them. Yes, I'm sorry
For those bricks and mortar, crashing joists
And ancient floorboards. Houses don't have feelings,
Do they? Lucky for us that they don't.

Ruining two centuries' handwork, Irish masons
Laid the stones. Irish work and Irish genius
Pissed on for a night of spite.

Still, it happened. It's forgotten,
It's remembered. Well, who cares?

Lord and Lady Simper-Footwell and the men
Who burned their mansion, all

Except your poor old Grandad,
Roast in hell, or roost in heaven. Give

Or take another five years, you can
Spread manure on
What's left. Fallen arches, twisted ivy,
Holes in walls that stood for pride.

Have another Guinness, Declan. I'd not
Rack your pretty head with bothering
About an old war. That, or any other. Drink, and smile.

To My Old Typewriter

L. C. Smith, 1918

You cost me five pounds in an Aylsham sale.
For over a decade you've served me well
And it's not your fault, if I have to stop.
My fingers won't divide; you're out of luck.
What earlier owners may have punched your keys
I've never known. I don't suppose I've cared.
For you were the nanny of my prime

And raised seven novels on your roller bar
And sent five books of poems ribboning
Through many drafts. You might send many more,
But not for me. I ask you to lie fallow
Across my office in memoriam
Of our twelve years together, yoked as one.
A willing workhorse at the study fire

You always waited, saddled up, ready to go
Over the fences when I caught the scent
Of a foxy piece of prose, or a foxy poem.
Yield to the tractor now. Your electric cousin
Plugged in the wall is all that I can manage.
Others may come one day, when I am dead,
And buy you cheaply, and perhaps treat you right

And give more business to your solid frame.
I hope so. As I touch your shift in sadness
I feel a tremor as of something moving
Anxious to work again, and be of use.
Lie still in dust. The time for iron will come.
The day of brass and modest wood will come.
An honest few will always honour you.

THE PRICE

Knowing that you are coming, and quite soon,
I sense the glory of the world unchanged.
The sun keeps rising. Sometimes even the moon
Comes up as if a birth has been arranged.

It has. Not more than seven months away,
You wave to me across the skinny hill
Where, bean-like, you grow strong. What must we pay
For something so conducive to good will?

Is there a price for what the cold stars bring
And lay in screaming wonder at our feet?
Some barter for our unformed gathering
That grows to raw flesh in the womb's white heat?

I think there is. An invoice for our joy
Whether you be my daughter, or a boy.

THE SICK

The sick are like the old. When muscles waste
They end as famished shadows of themselves.
Their skin goes cold, the colour of the paste
That seventies put on to look like twelves.

A second childhood comes. And then a third.
Steel wheel-chairs carry babies to their meals
Where eating means extrusion of a turd.
The costive athlete squirms on useless heels.

Imagine, then, the evening traffic jams
These dream of, where they idle, browse and talk,
The stirrup-cups they manage, the young lambs
They seem like when their mounted bodies walk.

Yes, walk. Some dream they walk again through a door,
Even dance a fox-trot on a slippery floor . . .

HOMES

You've seen them often, classical affairs
With porticoes and porches, grey and gaunt.
The inmates are – outside. In basket chairs
They're wheeled to take the sun, a kind of taunt.

Their future dwindles into fields of sheep
Under a sky of settling rain, then snow.
What gave them pleasure most returns in sleep
And warms their tongues, from churns of long ago.

Their palsied hands are shrunk. Their eyes implore
The blank horizon and the passing cows.
Pain infiltrates their bodies floor by floor.
Their brains are mortuary rooms that house

The corpses of what was, and what will be.
Then someone brings a trolley with their tea.

The Worst Fear

Some days I do feel better. Then I know
It couldn't come to this, it never would.
I'm much the same as I was long ago
When I could walk two thousand yards, and stand

Upright at parties, chatting. When the men
At petrol stations understood
The words I mouthed. Now is the same as then.
It isn't, though. These are the days when food

Falls from my grip, drink chokes me in my throat
And I'm a nervous nuisance, prone to tears.
The time has come when I put on my coat
With fumbling fingers, grappling with my fears

Of God knows what. Well, I know one that's worse
Than all the rest. My wife's become my nurse.

THE CONFINEMENT

I thought about the dwarf, Toulouse-Lautrec
Who lived with whores, and had his way with whores.
It wasn't just a kiss and then a neck.
He screwed them, and he gave them sores

That he'd inherited from other whores.
Life might be a confinement, you a wreck,
But why not satisfying? Why with bores?
Why live in some dull home, and drown in dreck?

Wasn't it better with the prostitutes
In a Victorian brothel, gold and red,
Where men came in to fuck in business suits
And no-one ever thought about being dead?

I wonder. It's the best at home in bed,
I think, arranged like spoons, my cheek against your head.

THE MIRROR

I watch an old man with a knotted, flamboyant tie
Walking on two sticks up the road. He looks
About twenty years older than me, very nearly eighty.

Sometimes he stops for a rest, stares up at the windows
Where younger people are laughing, blowing kisses to each other.
Sometimes he smiles, as if at a private joke.

I like this old man. I admire his slow progress
Towards an inevitable pause, perhaps for a drink.
I smile, and he smiles back. Life's funny, really.

There are days, though, when I can't match his aplomb.
I glare at the mirror. I want the glass to break
And let the young man out, who is inside, crying.

The Patients

There are five patients I have to tell you about.
Michael first, with his nid-nodding head
And his love of Christian names, Jason from Bedford
Who has twenty seconds' warning
Before his attacks – time to stop the car –
   And Roger who never smiles.

I mean, if you were Roger, penned in a chair
At the age of thirty-two, I wonder
If you would smile? Peter thinks not,
Painting the agile young Indian from Brixton
With his left hand, the only part
   Not affected by his disease.

'Do you still have erections?' they ask,
That 'still' hovering like the blade
Of the guillotine. Doctors are mean,
Mustapha thinks, whom they ask often
While they toy with the pit of his arm.
   An operation perhaps

Will carry Mustapha past forty. There remains
Colder comfort for the others. At home now
Soldiering on with my limp and my cough
I remember Michael and Jason, Roger and Peter
   And Mustapha,

Those foot soldiers in the long retreat
From the Moscow of getting well
   And I say a prayer:

Dear God, who created the human condition
And put the pain and death in the bottle,
Let there be scotch and water for those poor sinners
Who have no more hope, and a shot of morphine
   To carry them through.

THE PATIENT

Alive in the torture-chamber,
He stared at the flowers: the scent of freesia
Like a nerve gas, even the teddy bears
On his get-well card were leering.

It had been a fun week.
His head offered the claustrophobia of a box
And a pair of magnets, electrodes
Clamped to his wrists and ankles.

Rumour had it
They put the current through your balls
If you mentioned impotence.

Meanwhile, the doctors
Went round and round like clockwork,
Like the grand alliance against the Iraqis,
In the sand.

He refused the hara-kiri of a milligram,
Took the short cut to his death sentence,
And ate his dinner.

PHYSIO-THERAPY

A pretty girl limped in.
She lay down on her back
On the bed,
Wearing tights and a tank top.
She lifted her knees.

A second girl bent down between the first girl's knees,
Heels under her bottom.
She put her palms inside the first girl's thighs.

'Try to stop me opening your legs,' she said.

But the first girl couldn't, however much
She strained and cried.

All the men in wheel-chairs
Found it very erotic.

He remembered a gas-mask
That had lost its mother.

He heard the shrapnel squeal,
All the way to market.

Nobody cared. Nobody cares now, he thought,
As he lifted a dog-headed stick
In his wasted hand
And shook it at silence.

Egyptian gods came out of the woodwork
And squinted through him. But he paid no attention.

The wag-clock was ticking
Like a table-shelter. There had to be bombs,

For there to be peace. That was the principle
Most of us live by.

But the rest die, only slowly.

So he took up the hour-glass
Like a cyanide capsule
And crushed it between his teeth.

Crying wolf, once too often.

LIMITATIONS

You can watch a species improving itself. Take
The pied wagtail, for example. They make

Their sudden swoops and dips, then run on wheels
Looking for food. It all feels

Awfully like an unpredictable success
For the colours of black and white. No stress

On anything beyond a swift movement of wings
And an accurate dive on tarmac. Things

Are looking up for a world in which a pied wagtail
Can find what it needs without fail

By using only speed and intelligence.
Limitations of this kind make sense.

LIST OF SUBSCRIBERS

Anna Adams
Fergus Allen
K. N. Atkinson
Marlene Badger
Jonathan Barker
William Barklam
James Berry
Pamela Bigsby
John Bingham
David L. Bisset
Frank Brierley
Elizabeth Brock
Dennis Brown
Dr Stuart Bruce
Charlotte Brunsdon
Peter Chamberlain
Mrs G. E. Church
Alan Clodd
Michael and Barbara Copp
John Cotton
K. D. Craig
Andy Croft
Martyn Crucefix
Neil Curry
Peter Dale
E. Davies
Heather Davison
Gerald Dawe
Joan Deitch
Hugh Dickson

Patrick Drysdale
Carol Ann Duffy
Jane Duran
Alistair Elliot
Tony Ellis
Tim Ellis
Margo Ewart
Ruth Fainlight
Georgina Fekete
Duncan Forbes
Joy and Eric Francis
Judy Gascoyne
Giles Gordon
Chloë Greenwood
Gay Grossart
Paul Groves
D. H. W. Grubb
Harry Guest
Steven Halliwell
Alex Hamilton
Margaret and David Harrop
Anne Harvey
Noel Hayden
Cicely Herbert
Peter Hirschmann
Philip Hobsbaum
Hannah Hobsbaum-Kelly
Richard Holmes
Jeremy Hooker
Paul Hyland

Nicholas Johnson
Rosemary Jolly
Judith Kazantzis
Rosalind Kent
Mrs E. Lester
Mary Levinson
Penelope Lively
Edna Longley
Michael Longley
Penny MacBeth
Roger McGough
Ian McKelvie
Peter Meares
Dr Bernard Meehan
B. S. Meldrum
Adrian Mitchell
John Mole
Ralph Montagu
C. Morey de Morand
Blake Morrison
Madeline Munro
J. Nicholls
Michael O'Dell
Dennis O'Driscoll
Patrick O'Dwyer
Riana O'Dwyer
Masa Ohtake
Jeremy Page
Mario Petrucci

Peter Porter
Shahed Power
James Price
Jeremy Reed
Tom Rosenthal
Carol Rumens
Lawrence Sail
Vernon Scannell
Andrew J. Scott
Cecilia Scurfield
Amanda Sewell
Deirdre Shanahan
Dr Ann M. Soutter
Jon Stallworthy
Bernard Stone
Stephen Stuart-Smith
D. M. Thomas
Anthony and Ann Thwaite
Emily Thwaite
Shirley Toulson
Edward Upward
Edward Vanderpump
Robert Vas Dias
Len Webster
David Whiting
G. B. H. Wightman
Kit Wright
Pam Zinnemann-Hope